FU

A journal to destroy,
rant and vent without the
police getting involved

By Alex A. Lluch

WS Publishing Group
San Diego, California 92119

FU: A journal to destroy, rant and vent
without the police getting involved

By Alex A. Lluch
Published by WS Publishing Group
San Diego, California 92119
© Copyright 2009 by WS Publishing Group

Design by:
David Defenbaugh, Sarah Jang; WS Publishing Group

For more information on this and many other best-selling books visit
www.WSPublishingGroup.com.
E-mail: info@WSPublishingGroup.com

ISBN 13: 978-1-934386-62-0
Printed in China

Write a WARNING

on this page to anyone
who finds this book.

irr•i•ta•ting
transitive verb

1: to provoke impatience, anger,
or displeasure in : annoy
2: to induce irritability in or of
<I think your face is irritating>

annoy • bother • exasperate • irk • peeve • pester

Think of a person who **IRRITATES** you and complete the letter below.

Dear ....,

The sound of your voice reminds me of ....

.... When I see

your face I want to ....

.... You look like a ....

.... and smell like ....

The most annoying thing about you, however, is .....

....

....

If I could, I would tell you to ....

.... and throw ....at

you. I wish you would move to ....

.... for .... years.

chuck
verb

2 a: toss, throw
b: discard
c: dismiss, oust — used especially
with 'out'
<I was chucked out of work after I
threw this paper at someone>

toss • catapult • heave • throw • fling • lob

1 TEAR
out this page

2 CRUMPLE
it up

3 THROW
it at
someone

cuss
verb

1: to use profanely insolent
language against someone
<I am trying really hard not to
cuss you out>

p@#$k • b*&%$#d • s*&thead • c%&p • b&*$h

CUSSWORDS

Write down as many as you can think of.

Yell out your favorite as loud as you can!

rage
noun

1 a: violent and uncontrolled anger
b: a fit of violent wrath
2: violent action
3: an intense feeling : passion
<Traffic fills me with rage>

anger • frenzy • flare • rampage • rant • smolder

WHAT CONTRIBUTES TO YOUR FURY?

My ANGER!

LABEL THE BRANCHES OF THIS CHART

gar•bage
noun

1 a: food waste
b: discarded or useless material
c: inaccurate or useless data
<People should pay money to root
through my garbage>

litter • refuse • debris • rubbish • scrap • waste

TRASH

COLLAGE

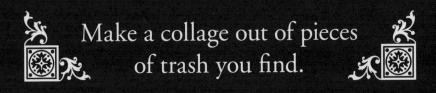

Make a collage out of pieces
of trash you find.

sign
noun

5 a: a display used to identify or
advertise a place of business or a
product
b: a posted command, warning,
or direction
<Heed my sign, or else>

be back later • closed • do not enter • beware of dog

IF
you could
stand on
the corner
with a
sign what
would it
say?

force
noun

3: violence, compulsion, or
constraint exerted upon or against
a person or thing
<Don't make me use force to show
you what's up>

assault • raid • strike • ravage • pounce • bombard

ATTACK

this page
with a

stapler

grate
verb

2: to cause irritation
<Your voice grates on my nerves>

gnash • rasping • harsh • noisy • rough • abrasive

EEEeeeeek!

Make a list
of every word
that sounds like
nails on a
chalkboard to you

gross
adjective

1 b: glaringly noticeable usually
because of inexcusable badness or
objectionableness
<I feel gross this morning>

 grumpy • disheveled • frumpy • groggy • unpleasant

Draw a picture of yourself when you WAKE UP on the WRONG SIDE of the bed.

ME

blow
noun

1 a: hard strike with a part of the
body or an instrument
<I would like to knock him out
with a blow to the face>

beat • bust • chop • clout • slug • sock • wallop

Make a list of
things you would like to

PUNCH

(Don't actually punch them.)

voo•doo
noun

2 a: a person who deals in spells
and necromancy
b: a sorcerer's spell
<Watch your back or I'll do
voodoo on you>

hex • curse • cast a spell • jinx • revenge • retribution

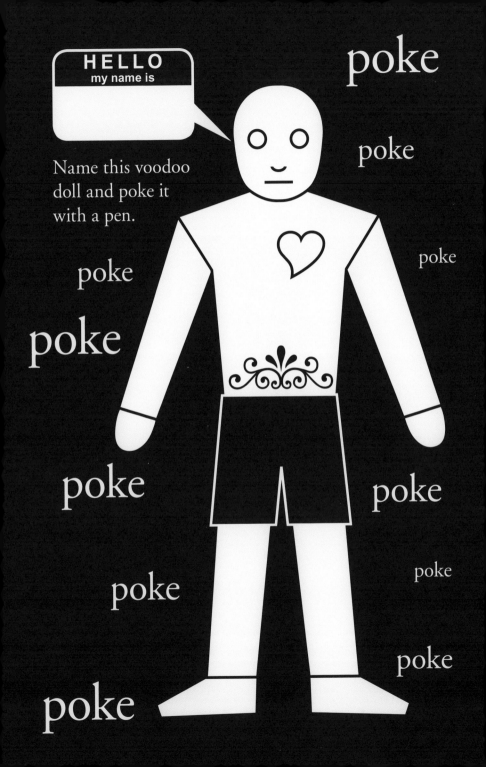

ev•i•dence
noun

1 b: something that
furnishes proof
<I can't deny the evidence that
you're a moron>

incriminate • threaten • intimidate • trouble • extort

Write down someone you would like to **B**LACKMAIL and what you would do.

piece
noun

RIP

1: a broken or irregular part of
something that often remains
incomplete
<I feel better after I destroy a piece
of this book>

tear • split • separate • divide • wrench • slash • pull

RIP

this page into as
many tiny pieces
as you can.

Throw them up
in the air like
confetti.

idiot
noun

2 a: foolish or stupid person
<I hope you learn to park, idiot>

blockhead • dolt • dummy • imbecile • moron • nitwit

FYI: Your parking sucks

Write a note to someone who has done a crappy parking job. Cut it out and keep it in your car for the next time you need it.

Dear Crappy
Parking Person,

tram•ple
verb

1: to tread heavily so as to bruise,
crush, or injure
<I want to trample on
my ex's dreams >

stamp • tromp • smash • squash • pound • crush • scuff

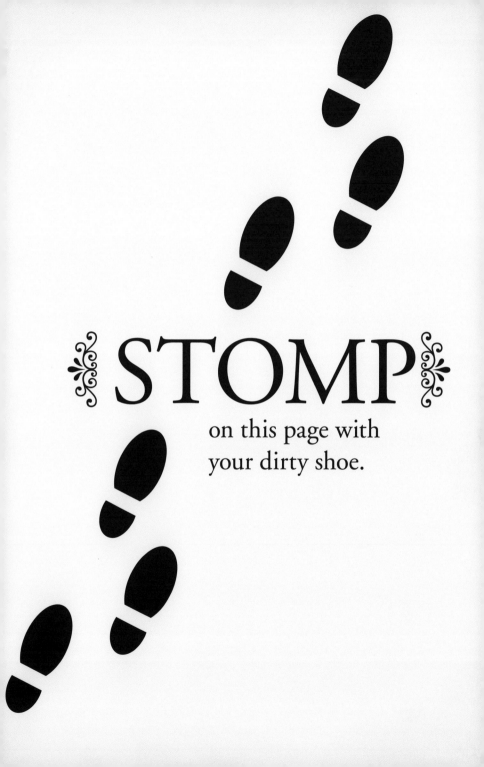

STOMP

on this page with
your dirty shoe.

des•e•crate
verb

2: to treat disrespectfully,
irreverently, or outrageously
<I will desecrate this journal>

defile • disfigure • contaminate • vandalize • mar • ruin

Your face would look
much better like this

 lue a picture of someone you can't stand here.
Then deface the picture — scribble, rip it,
draw horns or a moustache on it, etc.

break up
verb

1 a: to cease to exist as a unified
whole : disperse
b: to end a romance
<You suck so much I want to
break up with you>

separation • dissolution • divide • split • parting • finish

Write a
SCATHING LETTER
to an ex-girlfriend or ex-boyfriend.

D ear ....

....

....

....

....

....

....

....

....

....

....

....

shriek
verb

1: to utter a sharp shrill sound
2 a: to cry out in a high-pitched
voice
<Cover your ears before I shriek>

howl • screech • shriek • squeal • yelp • squawk • wail

Write down words that make you want to

SCREAM

Aaaaahhhhhhh!

Aaaaahhhhhhh!

py•ro•ma•nia
noun

1: an irresistible impulse
to start fires
<This journal DOES NOT
endorse pyromania>

blaze • combust • flame • glow • ignite • flare • radiate

If you could burn up one object, what would you choose?

....

BURN BABY, BURN

Don't really light it on fire.
Just use your imagination.

high•way rob•ber•y
noun

2: excessive profit or advantage
derived from a business
transaction
<The cost of this yacht is freakin'
highway robbery>

extravagant • overpriced • costly • steep • unreasonable

Paste a picture of
something that you're

PISSED
OFF

you will never be able
to afford here.

I CAN'T AFFORD THIS

happy
adjective

3 a: enjoying or characterized by
well-being and contentment
<The FU journal makes me
happy>

delighted • glad • joyful • ecstatic • elated • euphoric

Write down Positive Thoughts

(Yes, this can help too. Maybe.)

com•mu•ni•ca•tion
noun

Annoying
Email

3 a: a process by which information is
exchanged between individuals through
a common system of symbols, signs, or
behavior
<I say "FU" as a form of
communication>

notice • letter • message • note • memo • missive

You've received an

ANNOYING EMAIL

from your boss or coworker.

| | Send Now | Send Later | Delete | Priority |

Write what you *really* want to say in response.

....

....

....

....

....

....

....

....

....

....

You've got mail

kick-ass
adjective

1: to use forceful or coercive
measures in order to achieve a
purpose; also : to succeed or win
overwhelmingly: to kick butt
<This is a kick-ass journal>

amazing • awesome • incredible • extraordinary • sublime

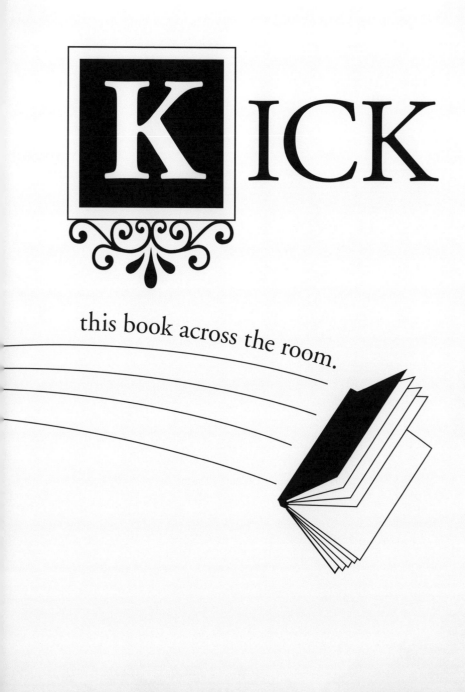

KICK

this book across the room.

vent
verb

1 c: to give often vigorous or
emotional expression to
<I will vent my frustrations on
this voodoo doll>

loose • release • unleash • rant • release • rage • mangle

smart al•eck
noun

1: an obnoxiously conceited
and self-assertive person with
pretensions to smartness or
cleverness
<This book lets me unleash my
inner smart aleck>

back talk • crack • quip • wisecrack • witticism • cut

Make a
list of your favorite
COMEBACKS

nui•sance
noun

1: one who is obnoxiously
annoying
<My in-laws are a nuisance>

noxious • bother • gadfly • gnawer • persecutor • pest

INSTRUCTIONS:
Have a friend write down what BUGS him or her about YOU on this page.

I have compiled this list of the varied reasons why

Y⚙️U
BUG

the crap out of me.*

Sincerely,

Sign & Date

* This may or may not represent a complete list of reasons why you bug the crap out of me.

pi•rate
noun

1: one who commits or
practices piracy
<Absolutely no pirates
allowed at my party>

forbid • exclude • prohibit • halt • reject • veto • restrain

You are

BLACKLISTED

ABSOLUTELY, UNDER NO CIRCUMSTANCES, SHOULD THESE INDIVIDUALS BE PERMITTED TO ATTEND MY BOMB@#S PARTY, THROWN SPECIFICALLY SO THEY CANNOT ATTEND

sar•casm
noun

1: a sharp and often satirical
or ironic utterance designed
to cut or give pain
<I am prone to bitter
sarcasm>

fake • false • guileful • insincere • phony • underhanded

Write a SARCASTIC apology letter for something you're not truly sorry for.

DEAR ....,

xoxo,

ME

spit
verb

1 a: to eject (as saliva) from
the mouth
<Excuse me while I spit
at you>

expectorate • spat • sputter • project • propel • hawk

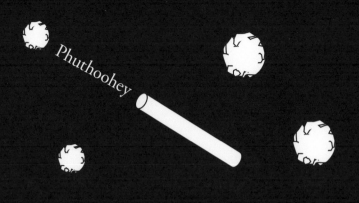

Phuthoohey

SPITballs

Make some
out of this
page.

Phuthoohey

work
noun

1: activity in which one
exerts strength or faculties to
do or perform something
<I prefer not to work today>

drudgery • grind • toil • labor • sweat • occupation

MY
company

RE: Office Policy
Dear Coworkers:

The following new and improved rules and regulations
will be effective immediately:

Your compliance is
appreciated.

Sincerely,
MANAGEMENT

List rules you would introduce or
change at your place of work.

primal scream therapy
noun

1: psychotherapy in which the patient
expresses normally repressed anger or
frustration especially through spontaneous and
unrestrained screams, hysteria, or violence.
<Don't mind my primal scream therapy>

therapeutic • remedy • cure • aid • help • relief • balm

FU 30-Second Therapy

STEP 1:
Open this book wide

STEP 2:
Hold it to your face

STEP 3:

scream
as loud as you can into this page

C'mon, you can scream louder than that!

en•e•my
noun

1: one that is antagonistic to another;
especially : one seeking to injure,
overthrow, or confound an opponent
<Stupid people are my enemy>

nemesis • bane • assailant • attacker • combatant • rival

rite a list of animals you wish would eat your

most hated enemy.

re•fuge
noun

1: shelter or protection from danger or distress
2: a place that provides shelter or protection
<I take refuge in a stiff cocktail>

harbor • haven • refuge • retreat • sanctuary • sanctum

Go to your
[H]appy place.

Paste cutouts from magazines here to make a collage of your happy place.

My Happy Place

Rorschach test
noun

1: a personality and intelligence test
in which a subject interprets inkblot
designs in terms that reveal intellectual
and emotional factors
<I failed the Rorschach test miserably>

conceive • imagine • realize • envision • contemplate

FIRST THOUGHTS

Write down the first things that come to mind...

Traffic: ....

Long lines at a store: ....

Barking dogs: ....

Getting a parking ticket: ....

Your job: ....

Politics: ....

Taxes: ....

Your landlord: ....

The DMV: ....

Being on hold: ....

People who chew with their mouth open: ....

Junk mail: ....

scratch
verb

3: to write or draw hastily or carelessly
<My boss makes me want to scratch
my eyes out>

claw • scrawl • doodle • scrape • grind • grate • sketch

SCRIBBLE

on this page as hard as you can.

ex•as•per•ate
verb

1 a: to excite the anger of : enrage
b: to cause irritation or annoyance to
<Crappy drivers exasperate me>

aggravate • incense • nettle • provoke • peeve • pissed

the fnger

Describe the last time you flipped someone off.

et•y•mol•o•gy   FU
noun

1: the history of a linguistic form
shown by tracing its development
since its earliest recorded
occurrence in language
<FU has its etymology in Latin>

fresh • novel • original • unheard-of • unprecedented

FU DICTIONARY

Make up your own brand-new cussword.

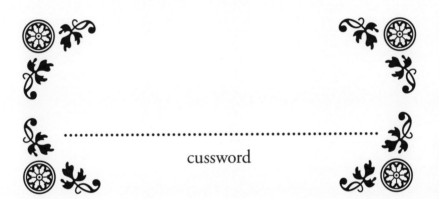

....

cussword

Now use it in a sentence:

....

....

....

....

....

....

gen•der vs.
noun

1 b: the behavioral, cultural,
or psychological traits typically
associated with one sex
<I can't figure out what the F is
wrong with the opposite gender>

gal • guy • girl • boy • woman • man • female • male

Make a list of things you hate about the 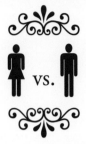 opposite sex.

shit
noun

1: usually vulgar : a worthless,
offensive, or detestable person
<My landlord is shit because he
raised my rent>

contemptible • despicable • detestable • dishonorable

If you could smash any electronic or appliance with a baseball bat, which would you choose?

< Your program has unexpectedly shut down >

skill
noun

1 b: dexterity or coordination
especially in the execution of
learned physical tasks
<I have some serious art skill>

creativity • ingenuity • inventiveness • talent • finesse

FU ART PROJECT

Place your hand on this page with your
middle finger raised and trace; then decorate.

im•pa•tient
adjective

1: restless or short of temper
especially under irritation, delay, or
opposition
<Waiting makes me freakin'
impatient>

complaining • fussing • griping • grumbling • whining

Sh*tty Business Bureau

Think about the last company that gave you terrible customer service. Tell them off here.

Thank you for calling. All customer service representatives are currently assisting other callers. You will be on hold for approximately 126 hours.

lie
verb

1: to make an untrue statement
with intent to deceive
2: to create a false or misleading
impression
<I caught him in a terrible lie>

fabrication • falsehood • fib • tale • untruth • whopper

What is the LAMEST LIE

you have ever been told?

Call that person out here.

ego•tism
noun

1 a: excessive use of the first person
singular personal pronoun b: the practice
of talking about oneself too much
2: an exaggerated sense of self-importance
<My friend's egotism is unbearable>

conceited • self-centered • self-important • stuck-up

cre•ate
verb

1: to make or bring into existence
something new
<I can create something beautiful>

assemble • construct • erect • fabricate • make • piece

Tear out this page.

Do something constructive with it (paper airplane, origami, etc).

spell
noun

1 a: spoken word or set of words
believed to have magic power
<I cast a spell on him; he will now
turn into a pig>

hex • conjuring • magic • mojo • sorcery • wizardry • jinx

CAST A SPELL

Use the incantation below to say FU to someone who deserves it. No wizarding experience needed.

INSTRUCTIONS:

- Clip a lock of your hair and place it in a bowl
- Pour in ½ cup of wine (red or white)
- Add 2 pinches of salt
- Stir counterclockwise
- Chant person's name 6 times

Now, check off which effect you want the spell to have on your foe.

☐ Have toes as fingers

☐ Grow excessive body hair

☐ Smell like raw onions

☐ Make all foods taste like dirt

☐ Inexplicable fear of cute baby animals

in•fam•ous
adjective

1: having a reputation
of the worst kind
<The heiress is infamous for
annoying the crap out of people>

notorious • contemptible • despicable • detestable • dirty

celebrities

who annoy the crap out of you

List 'em here and why they suck.

mot•to
noun

1: a sentence, phrase, or word
inscribed on something as
appropriate to or indicative of its
character or use
<I try to chant my motto
before I freak out>

slogan • aphorism • byword • epigram • maxim • proverb

My Motto

Write down your words to live by.

....

....

....

....

....

....

The next time you get pissed off,
think of these words.

mis•for•tune
noun

1 a: an event that causes an
unfortunate or distressing result : bad
luck
2: an unfortunate incident or event
<I sometimes wish my
enemies misfortune>

rotten luck • calamity • mishap • unpleasantness

FU fortune cookie

What fortune cookie you would like to pass out to people you can't stand?

Your fortune:

bulls•eye
noun

3 a: the center of a target
b: something that precisely attains
a desired end
<I hit my office mate with a
spitball: bullseye>

victory • success • mission accomplished • on the nose

Bullseye

Draw a picture of the most irritating person or thing in your life.

Then tear out this page, hang it on the wall, and throw darts at it.

black sheep
noun

1: a disfavored or disreputable
member of a group
<He is the black sheep of my
family because he's such a mooch>

bum • outcast • loafer • pariah • punk • reject

We're related?

Write an open letter to a relative who you would like removed from your family tree.

Dear,

fraud
noun

2 a: a person who is not what he or
she pretends to be
b: impostor
<The senator proved to be a fraud>

charlatan • cheat • crook • phony • snake • trickster

FU politics

What one person in politics would you like to lock in a room full of rabid dogs?

NO EXIT

MY NAME IS:

....

si•lence (mute)
noun

2: absence of sound or noise :
stillness
<I wish for complete silence
but never get it>

censor • hush • blackout • quiet • peace • clam up

SHUT
UP!

Open this page; point it at someone.

bud•dy
noun

1: companion, partner or friend
<I am not your buddy
because you suck>

mate • fellow • chum • coworker • pal • sidekick

FU_{space}

For people
who suck

Fill out this social networking profile for an enemy.

Name:

(Draw face here)

Motto:

Status:

Nickname:

Mood:

Music:

Interests:

Choose a URL:

hos•tage
noun

2: a person or thing taken by force
to secure the taker's demands
<I am holding her cat hostage until
she does the dishes>

captive • pawn • prisoner • token • security

IF YOU EVER EVER WANT
to SeE YOUR StaPlER...

A a a a A B b b C c c D d
d E E e E E F F f G g g H
h h I i í I I i J J j K K k L
l M m m N n n o o o O
o P p P Q q q R r r S s S
s T t T T u U U u U V v V
W w w X x x Y y y Z Z z
1 2 3 4 5 6 7 8 9 0 = + "
" ! @ # $ % ^ & * ? ( ) , .

Cut out letters to make a ransom-style note and
leave it for your roommates or coworkers to see

de•face
noun

1: to mar the appearance of : injure
by effacing significant details
2: destroy
<I enjoyed the chance
to deface this book>

mar • mangle • blemish • pelt • drub • wreck

Vandalize

this page with
4-letter words

fan•ta•sy
noun

5: the power or process of creating
especially unrealistic or improbable
mental images
<Being a millionaire
proved to be only a fantasy>

hallucination • fancy • dream • delusion • imagination

Poof

A genie appears and grants you 3 wishes to help improve your life.

What do you wish for?

1

2

3

es•cape
verb

1: to get away
2: to avoid a threatening evil
<I need to escape from this job>

bail • bolt • evade • emerge • run • elude

FU Bailout

This card will help you get away with something, like ditching work or a family reunion.

Present this card when needed.

GET OUT OF JAIL FREE

Cut out this card and keep it with you in case this occasion ever arises.

taunt
verb

1: to reproach or challenge in a
mocking or insulting manner
<Don't taunt me on a Monday
before my coffee>

barb • jeer • tease • insult • slam • slap

HERE IS YOUR EX'S HOUSE.
Tag it with all the mean names you'd
love to call that person to his or her face.

ar•tist
noun

2: a person skilled in creative
activity
<I am a wonderful artist. Not>

craftsman • virtuoso • creative • whiz • artisan

PAINT

this entire page with a
bottle of nail polish or
White Out.

re•lax
verb

1: to get rid of nervous
tension or anxiety
<This book has helped me relax.
Maybe>

rest • alleviate • comfort • ease • relieve • calm • cool